DK SUPER World

BRAZIL

From the Amazon rainforest to the
samba-filled streets of Rio de Janeiro,
take an exciting adventure through Brazil

DK Learning

PRODUCED FOR DK BY

Editorial Caroline Wakeman Literary Agency
Design Collaborate Agency
Graphic story illustrator Matt Garbutt

Project Editor Amanda Eisenthal
Senior Art Editor Gilda Pacitti
Managing Editor Carine Tracanelli
Managing Art Editor Sarah Corcoran
Production Editor Robert Dunn
Production Controller Rebecca Parton
Publisher Sarah Forbes
Managing Director, Learning Hilary Fine

First published in Great Britain in 2025
by Dorling Kindersley Limited
20 Vauxhall Bridge Road,
London SW1V 2SA

The authorised representative in the EEA is
Dorling Kindersley Verlag GmbH. Arnulfstr.
124, 80636 Munich, Germany

Copyright © 2025 Dorling Kindersley Limited
A Penguin Random House Company
10 9 8 7 6 5 4 3 2 1
001–345886–Jun/2025

A CIP catalogue record for this book
is available from the British Library.
ISBN 978-0-2417-2670-9

Printed and bound in China

www.dk.com

This book was made with Forest
Stewardship Council™ certified
paper – one small step in DK's
commitment to a sustainable future.
**Learn more at www.dk.com/uk/
information/sustainability**

CONTENTS

MAP   4
Brazil

FACT FILE   6
All About Brazil

TERRAINS   8
Rainforests, Rivers and Wetlands

LANDMARKS   10
Iguaçu Falls

FLORA AND FAUNA   12
Amazonian Animals and Super Predators

CULTURE   18
Diversity, Entertainment and Sports

RELIGION   22
Catholicism, Candomblé and Shamanism

NATIONAL HOLIDAYS AND FESTIVALS   24
Light, Colour, Carnival!

FOOD AND DRINK   26
Stews, Seafood and Sweet Treats

RECIPE   28
Brigadeiros

HOME, WORK AND SCHOOL   30
Cities, Schools and Industry

SCHOOL DAY DIARY   32
Izabela's Day

HISTORY   36
Colonisation, Freedom, Democracy

HOW NIGHT CAME FROM THE OCEAN   38

VOCABULARY BUILDER   42
Fruits of Brazil

GLOSSARY   44

INDEX   46

Words in **bold** are explained in the glossary on page 44.

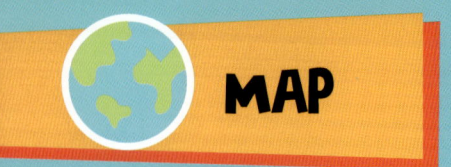

BRAZIL

Brazil is the largest country in South America. It is home to the world's biggest **rainforest**: the Amazon. Brazil has vibrant wildlife, landscapes, food and celebrations. It is split into 26 states and one **federal district.**

Roraima

Amapá

Tocantins

Rio Grande do Norte

Maranhão

Paraíba

Amazonas

Pará

Pernambuco

Ceará

Alagoas

Acre

Piauí

Sergipe

Mato Grosso

Bahia

Rondônia

Brasília, Federal District

Goiás

Minas Gerais

Mato Grosso do Sul

Espírito Santo

São Paulo

Paraná

Rio de Janeiro

Santa Catarina

Rio Grande do Sul

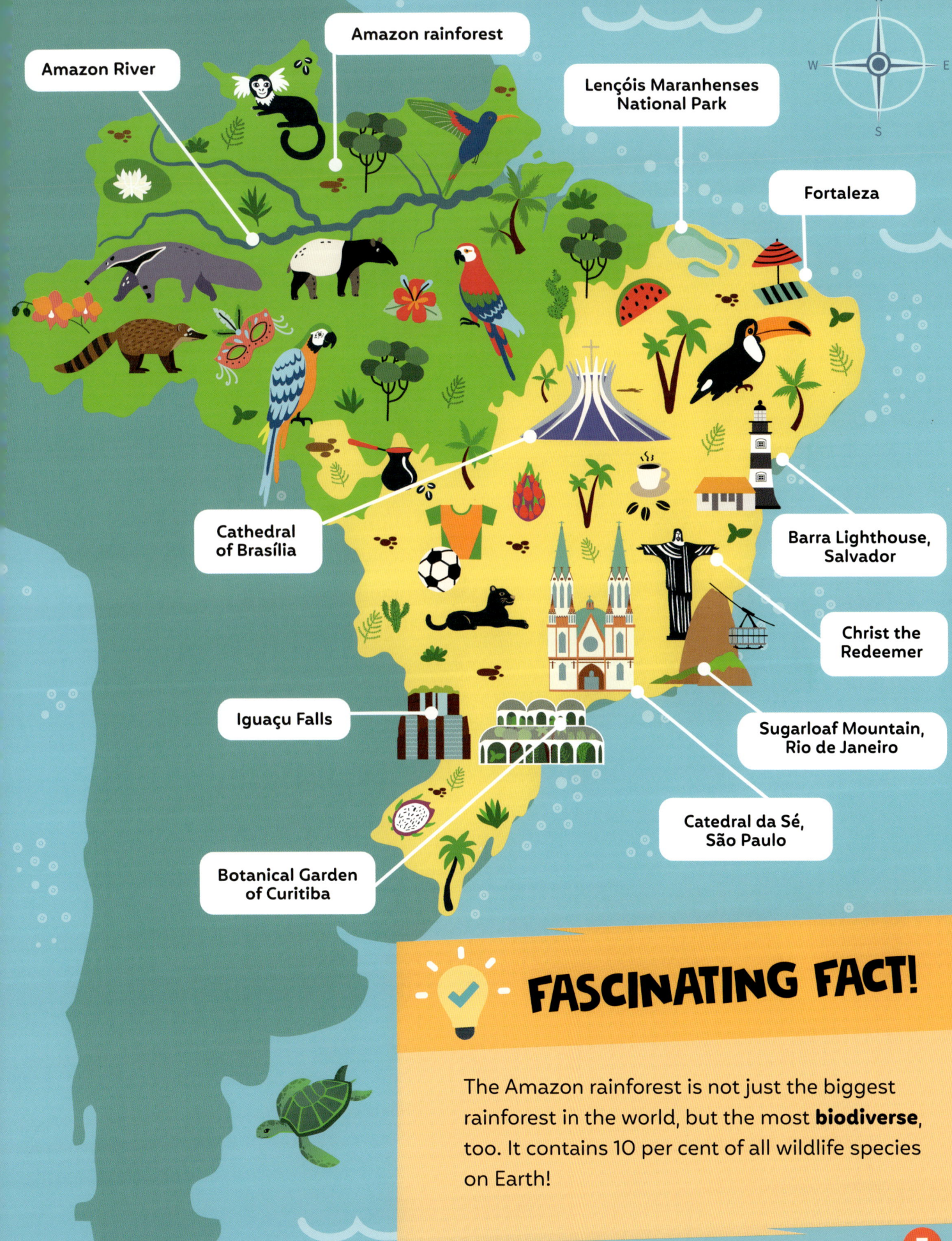

Amazon River

Amazon rainforest

Lençóis Maranhenses National Park

Fortaleza

Cathedral of Brasília

Barra Lighthouse, Salvador

Christ the Redeemer

Iguaçu Falls

Sugarloaf Mountain, Rio de Janeiro

Botanical Garden of Curitiba

Catedral da Sé, São Paulo

FASCINATING FACT!

The Amazon rainforest is not just the biggest rainforest in the world, but the most **biodiverse**, too. It contains 10 per cent of all wildlife species on Earth!

FACT FILE

ALL ABOUT BRAZIL

Bandeira do Brasil

🏳 Flag: Bandeira do Brasil

⌖ Capital city: Brasília

👤 Population: Approx. 216 million

💬 Official language: Portuguese

💵 Currency: Real R$

🌳 National tree: Pau-brasil, also called Brazilwood

⬤ National dish: Feijoada

🐦 National bird: Rufous-bellied thrush

🎵 National anthem: "Hino Nacional Brasileiro" ("Brazilian National Anthem")

☆ Major exports: Soybeans, corn, sugar, petroleum

FASCINATING FACT!

The rufous-bellied thrush helps the rainforests to grow. It eats ripe fruits and then spits out the seeds, planting new fruit trees.

Capital city

Brasília is the third biggest city in Brazil. It is where the Brazilian government is based. Brasília was built in 1956 specifically to be the capital city. Before that, the capital was Rio de Janeiro on the coast.

States and stars

There are 26 states in Brazil, plus one Federal District for the capital city. For this reason, there are 27 stars on the Brazilian flag. The words on the flag are "*Ordem e Progresso*", which means "Order and Progress". This is the national motto.

Language

Brazil is the only South American country that speaks Portuguese. Brazilian Portuguese is pronounced differently to European Portuguese, and some of the terms are different. For example, in Portugal, "train" is *comboio*, while in Brazil, it's *trem.*

Equator

FIND OUT!

Brazil is so big it shares a border with every other country in South America except two. Can you name these two countries?

Answer: Chile and Ecuador

Equatorial land

Brazil is mostly in the Southern **Hemisphere** just below the **equator**. In the Southern Hemisphere, the summers last from about December to March and the winters last from June to September.

RAINFORESTS, RIVERS AND WETLANDS

Brazil is the fifth-biggest country in the world. It has **tropical** climates in the north and **subtropical** climates further south. This allows for varied terrains, from vast rainforests to long coasts, and marshy **wetlands** to dry savannahs.

Amazon rainforest

The Amazon rainforest has almost 400 billion trees. **Ecologically**, the Amazon is incredibly important, as it is home to millions of species of plants and animals. It also absorbs more than 40 per cent of all the **carbon dioxide** in the world.

Amazon River

The Amazon River is the second longest river on Earth. During the wet season, the river can be up to 50 kilometres (31 miles) wide! The river runs right through the Amazon rainforest from east to west. It is joined by around 1,100 **tributaries** before it drains into the Atlantic Ocean.

Wetlands

The Pantanal is a vast tropical wetland of about 210,000 square kilometres (81,000 sq miles) – that's twice the size of Iceland. Each year, the Pantanal fills up during rainy season and slowly drains away during the dry season. It's a refuge for around 10 million **caimans**.

Savannah

The Cerrado in central Brazil is the most biodiverse savannah in the world. A savannah is a shrubby plain of grassland with scattered trees. It gets dry winters and rainy summers, which makes it an excellent place for varied plant life. However, nearly half of the Cerrado vegetation is lost due to over-farming.

FASCINATING FACT!

A new animal or plant species is found in the Amazon rainforest an average of once every other day.

Coasts

Brazil's 7,491-kilometre (4,654-mile) coastline along the Atlantic Ocean has some of the most famous, and longest, golden sandy beaches in the world. On the coast in the north, you'll find the unique Lençóis Maranhense National Park, with rolling white sand dunes and lagoons of emerald-green water.

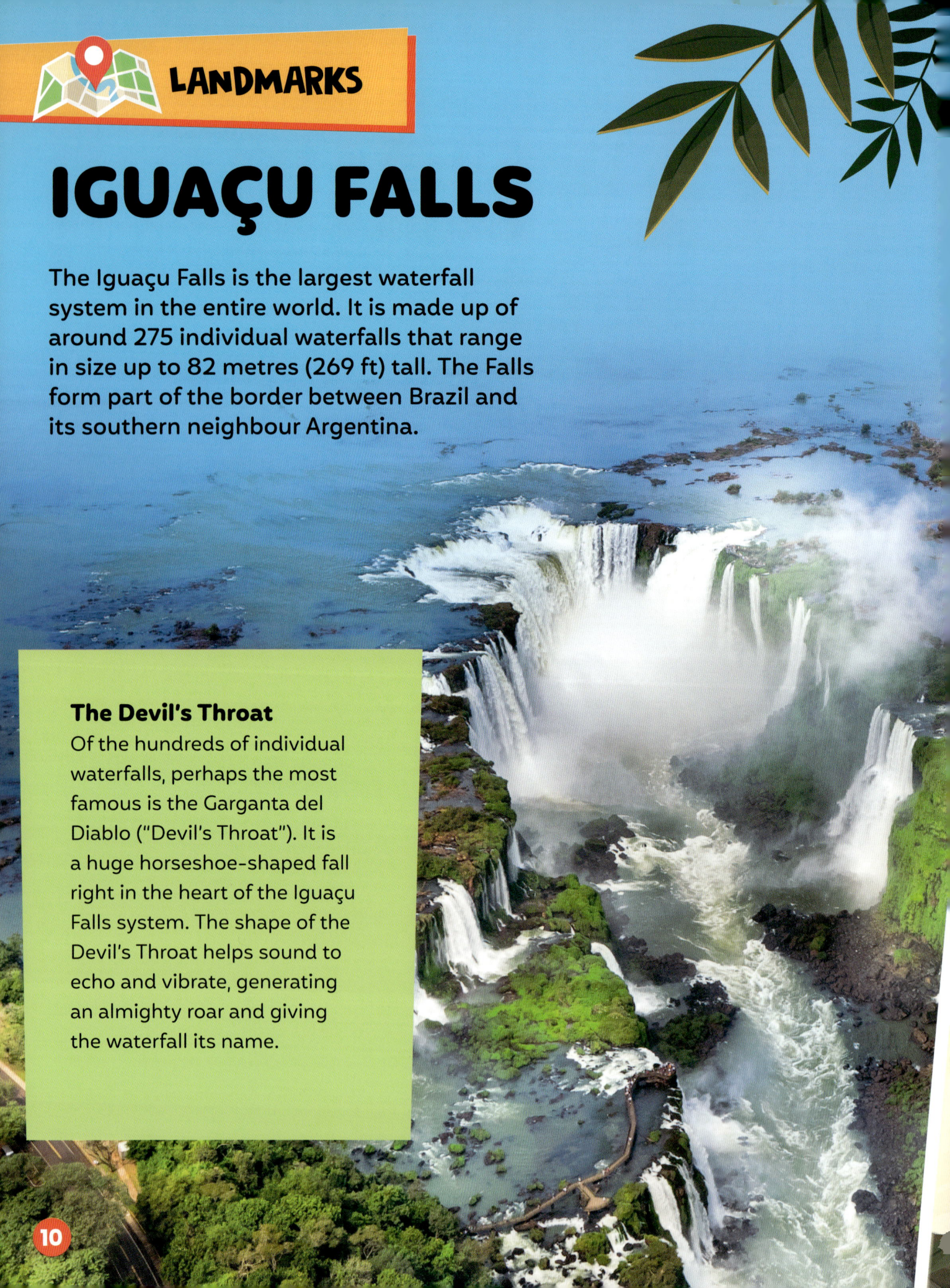

IGUAÇU FALLS

The Iguaçu Falls is the largest waterfall system in the entire world. It is made up of around 275 individual waterfalls that range in size up to 82 metres (269 ft) tall. The Falls form part of the border between Brazil and its southern neighbour Argentina.

The Devil's Throat

Of the hundreds of individual waterfalls, perhaps the most famous is the Garganta del Diablo ("Devil's Throat"). It is a huge horseshoe-shaped fall right in the heart of the Iguaçu Falls system. The shape of the Devil's Throat helps sound to echo and vibrate, generating an almighty roar and giving the waterfall its name.

Formation of the Falls

Millions of years ago, volcanoes erupted over a desert to form the Paraná Plateau: a surface of extremely hard **basaltic** rock over layers of very soft **sandstone**. Movements in the earth formed cracks, and the Iguaçu River flowed through those cracks. This **eroded** the softer rock while the hard basaltic rock formed steep cliffs.

Hard rock

Soft rock

Steep cliffs form

Water erodes the soft rock

FASCINATING FACT!

The splashing water of the Falls creates a mist of rainbows 150 metres (500 ft) high.

Parks and wildlife

Besides the waterfalls, Iguaçu National Park has hundreds of kilometres of rainforests and other wild land. The park has an abundance of wildlife, including animals that are rarely seen elsewhere, like giant anteaters and jaguarundis. It also has more than 600 species of butterfly!

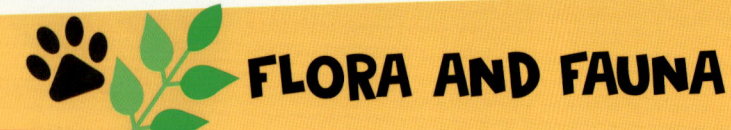

AMAZONIAN ANIMALS AND SUPER PREDATORS

Brazil has some of the most diverse wildlife of any natural space. New species are being found all the time. Unfortunately, due to **deforestation** and the farming **industry**, wild habitats are under threat.

IN THE TREETOPS

Hyacinth macaw

Toco toucan

At 60 centimetres (2 ft) long, these big birds are the largest toucan species. Their curved orange beaks are almost a third of their body length. When they sleep, they tuck their beaks under their wings to keep warm. Toucans are not great flyers, so they mostly hop about in the treetops.

Harpy eagle

These raptors are so strong they can snatch sloths and monkeys from the rainforest canopy and carry them off. Their eyesight is eight times better than a human's, and they are so agile they can fly through the treetops at 80 kilometres per hour (50 mph) .

Golden lion tamarin

These tiny monkeys are **endemic** to the Atlantic forests of Brazil. They are about the size of a squirrel and have bright golden fur and a tufted mane. Golden lion tamarins live in small family groups. They forage mainly on fruits, insects and small mammals.

Maned sloth

These sloths have three toes and a long black mane. Maned sloths are very slow creatures that travel an average of just 38 metres (125 ft) a day. They are rare, found only in the coastal forests of Brazil. Their habitat is under constant threat from deforestation. To safely hang upside down for long periods of time, special blood vessels help pump oxygen, and their organs are attached to their ribs so they don't get squashed.

WATERY WILDLIFE

Yacaré caiman

Caiman

Yacaré and spectacled caimans are found in huge numbers in the Pantanal wetlands. They are the favourite prey of ferocious jaguars. The yacaré males are about 2.5 metres (8 ft) and spectacled males about 2 metres (6.5 ft). The females are slightly smaller.

Red-bellied piranha

These Amazonian fish have sharp, interlocking teeth that give them a powerful bite. They are mainly scavengers and eat small fish, insects, plants and seeds. In rare cases, they can swarm in groups to take down larger animals that are sick or injured.

Pink river dolphin

Also known as *boto*, these dolphins are found only in the Amazon. The bulb on their heads helps them use **echolocation** to hunt fish in the muddy Amazon waters. Their thin, sharp teeth can crack open turtle shells.

Giant Amazon waterlily

Victoria amazonica have platform-like leaves that float on the water. They can reach 3 metres (10 ft) across and can support the weight of a golden retriever. The undersides of the pads trap air to help them float.

Anaconda

These snakes live both in the water and on the land. The heaviest anaconda ever recorded weighed 227 kilograms (500 lb)! That's as much as a full-grown tiger. They are constrictors, which means they hunt by wrapping their bodies around their prey to suffocate them.

Capybara

These are the biggest rodents in the world, measuring up to 1.4 metres (4.6 ft) long! They wallow in the Pantanal and have webbed toes for swimming. Their eyes are high on their heads so they can check above the water for danger.

Human
1.7 metres (5.6 ft)

Yacaré caiman
2.5 metres (8 ft)

Anaconda
6 metres (20 ft)

Capybara
1.4 metres (4.6 ft)

Jaguar
1.8 metres (6 ft)

Spectacled caiman
2 metres (6.5 ft)

Waterlily
3 metres (10 ft)

RAINFOREST WILDERNESS

Giant anteater

At more than 2 metres (6.5 ft) long, giant anteaters have to eat tens of thousands of ants a day to survive! They have no teeth but use their huge claws to dig at ant and termite nests. A 60-centimetre (2-foot) long tongue snatches out ants.

Brazil nut tree

These trees have a **mutualistic relationship** with rodents called agouties who have sharp teeth that break into the tough shell of the nuts. Agouties then store the nuts for future. The ones they forget about become new trees.

Jaguar

These large cats are deadly hunters. They are strong swimmers and live in tropical forests near water. They hunt ground animals like armadillos, deer and monkeys, as well as water prey like caimans and turtles. Their powerful jaws can bite through bone and shells.

ENDANGERED SPECIES

Deforestation

Palicourea elata is better known as "hot lips" because the bright red leaves grow in the shape of a pair of lips. Deforestation for the farming industry has caused the plant to become **endangered**. It is medicinal and can treat rashes, earaches and coughs.

Pollution

Giant otters are sleek, playful mammals native to the Amazon River and Pantanal wetlands. They are hunters who play a key role in the **ecosystem**, but they are also reducing in number. Much of this is due to pollution in the water from mining and agriculture.

Habitat loss

Maned wolves have long legs and a black mane that stands on end when they feel threatened. Maned wolf **populations** are in decline because so much of their grassland and rainforest habitats are cleared and used for farmland.

DIVERSITY, ENTERTAINMENT AND SPORTS

Brazilian culture is a rich mix. Its deep history involves Indigenous peoples, Portuguese **colonisation**, a long trade in **enslaved** people from Africa, and immigration from around the world. Today, almost half the population identify as mixed-race. All of this has led to a huge variety of music, dance, food and customs.

FASCINATING FACT!

Brazil has the largest Japanese population outside of Japan itself.

DIVERSITY

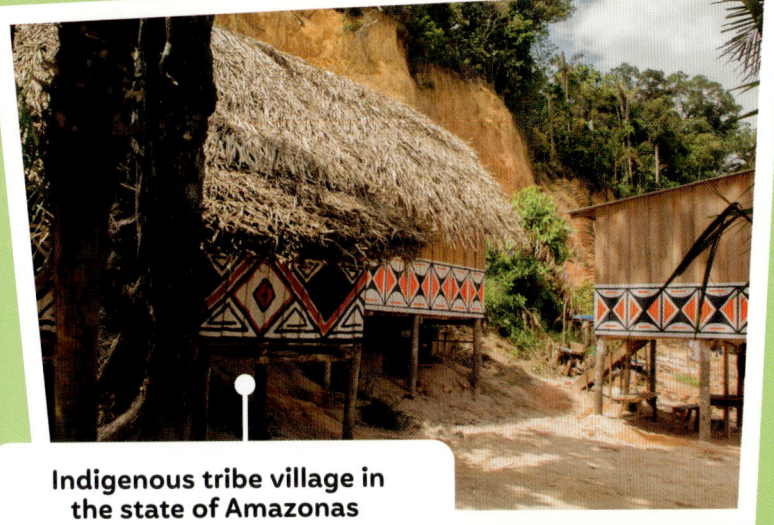

Indigenous tribe village in the state of Amazonas

Indigenous

There are around 1.7 million Indigenous people living in Brazil. Indigenous communities have a huge variety of languages, customs, beliefs and lifestyles. The largest group is the Guaraní. Almost all of their land has been lost and stolen since European colonisation.

African

African influences are everywhere! African spices and techniques are used for cooking classic Brazilian dishes. Afro-Brazilian dances and music styles like samba are very popular. The colours, costumes and customs in celebrations like Carnival have deep African influences.

Portuguese-style architecture in the Pelourinho district of Salvador, Bahia

European

About 45 per cent of the population identify as white with European **heritage.** European roots are mostly Portuguese, but there are also strong German and Italian connections. The European influence can be seen in the Portuguese language, architecture, customs and love of football.

19

ENTERTAINMENT

Telenovelas

This is a kind of TV programme that's enormously popular in Brazil. The programmes are set in the real world and often have dramatic, emotional plots and a familiar cast of characters. There is a focus on romance and family, and on revealed secrets!

Samba

Samba is both a type of dance and a type of music. It originated with enslaved African communities. Dancers wear vivid colours and feathered headdresses. The dance involves rapid foot and hip movements led by African drumming rhythms. Samba is especially important at the Carnival festival.

Beach life!

Brazil has some of the most famous beaches in the world, like Copacabana and Ipanema. People will arrive early and spend their whole day at the beach. They might chat with friends, surf, play volleyball and eat and drink at the many beach kiosks.

SPORTS

Capoeira

This is a martial art in which fighting movements are performed to music and drumming. It was invented by enslaved Africans to disguise the fact that they were practising self-defence. After slavery was **abolished** in 1888, the government found capoeira so threatening they made it illegal for 40 years!

Futebol!

Football, or *futebol* in Portuguese, is the nation's favourite sport. Brazil has won the FIFA World Cup more times than any other country. Football was introduced by Scottish immigrants in the late 1800s. Since then, Brazil has been football mad.

Mixed martial arts

This sport, known as MMA, combines techniques from various fighting styles. In Brazil, the main techniques come from Brazilian jiu-jitsu, where the focus is on grappling. MMA fighters are also skilled in kickboxing, karate, wrestling and more.

CATHOLICISM, CANDOMBLÉ AND SHAMANISM

Catholicism is the main religion of Brazil, brought over by the Portuguese. The religions Candomblé and Umbanda are uniquely Afro-Brazilian and stem from enslaved communities.
The hundreds of Indigenous communities all have their own beliefs and practices.

Catholicism

Catholicism is a type of Christianity. Christians worship Jesus Christ, the son of an almighty god. Catholics also follow the Pope, a spiritual leader based in Rome. Catholics believe that confessing your sins will allow God to forgive you. Catholic religious rituals are called sacraments.

Catedral da Sé

Candomblé

Candomblé is an Afro-Brazilian religion that stemmed from African beliefs. Followers worship *orixás*: spirits of nature and human life, such as thunder, family and love. Oludumaré is the supreme creator, and Yemanjá is the goddess of the sea. Candomblé ceremonies are full of music and dancing.

 FASCINATING FACT!

Enslaved people had to hide their Candomblé faith, which was made illegal until the 1970s. They had to pretend to be Catholics and incorporate Catholic icons in their worship.

A statue of Yemanjá

Umbanda

This Afro-Brazilian religion blends African beliefs with Catholic and Indigenous elements. Umbanda has *orixás* alongside Indigenous spirits, Catholic saints, spirits of past enslaved people and a god called Olorun.

Shamanism and spiritualism

Religions and beliefs in Indigenous tribes are diverse and varied. Some might worship spirits that inhabit animals and elements of nature. Many tribes also have shamans: holy people who act as advisors, healers and scholars. Shamans sometimes communicate between the human and spiritual worlds.

Rituals and ceremonies

Indigenous peoples have many practices. In the Ticuna tribe, when girls reach a certain age, they dance over fires for days before learning their people's history. Shamans of the Awá tribe use clapping and chanting to go into a trance and commune with the spirits.

LIGHT, COLOUR, CARNIVAL!

Brazil is a country that loves to celebrate! Their holidays and festivals are often vibrant and colourful, full of music and dancing.

Carnival (Carnaval do Brasil)

Held in spring, Carnival is the biggest festival in Brazil. It is celebrated with five days of parties, music, dancing, sparkly costumes and food and drink. There are huge parades of samba dancers in feathery costumes, and even the spectators dress up!

Rio Carnival parade

FIND OUT!

The biggest Carnival celebration is in Rio de Janeiro, where millions of people take part. Can you find out what state Rio de Janeiro is in?

Answer: Rio de Janeiro state!

Black Consciousness Day
(Dia da Consciência Negra)

20 November honours Brazil's Afro-Brazilian population. It is a day to celebrate the culture, history and community of Afro-Brazilians and to recognise the struggles of Black communities. The date honours Zumbi dos Palmares, a formerly enslaved person who fought to abolish slavery.

Independence Day
(Dia da Independência)

On 7 September, Brazilians celebrate the anniversary of Brazil's independence from Portugal, beginning in 1822. People take part in parades and enjoy fireworks.

Corpus Christi

60 days after Easter, Brazilians celebrate the Christian holiday of Corpus Christi. People make carpets called *tapetes de rua* to decorate the streets. Different cities use different materials, including flowers, coloured sawdust, embroidery, sand and even coffee.

Bonfim Stairs Washing
(Lavagem do Bonfim)

In Salvador, on the second Thursday of January, people dressed in white walk 8 kilometres (5 miles) to the Church of Nosso Senhor do Bonfim. Baianas (Afro-Brazilian women from Bahia) carry jars of water and wash the steps of the church. The celebration has elements of both Catholic and Afro-Brazilian cultures.

25

STEWS, SEAFOOD AND SWEET TREATS

Brazilian cuisine is a blend of influences from Indigenous, African and European peoples. There is a wide variety of flavours, aromas and textures. Dishes from particular regions reflect local traditions.

Cassava

Also known as yuca, tapioca and manioc, this is a root vegetable used in a lot of Brazilian cooking. Some popular forms are cassava chips, mashed cassava and *farofa* – a side dish made from toasted cassava flour.

Farofa

Feijoada

This is a stew of black beans and meats cooked slowly over a few hours. It is considered Brazil's national dish. The name comes from the Portguese *feijão* meaning beans.

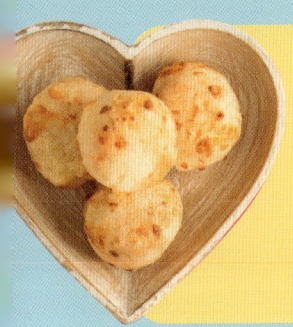

Pão de queijo

The name translates to "cheese bread". These are small balls of soft white bread filled with cheese. Cassava flour is used, which gives the balls a bit of a chew and a crunch!

Brigadeiro

This is a classic Brazilian treat! It is made with chocolate powder, butter and condensed milk, rolled into a ball and coated in chocolate sprinkles.

Guaraná

This is an energy drink made from the seeds of the guaraná plant. The Sateré-Mawé people of the Amazon were the first to farm it and make a drink called *çapó*.

Moqueca

This is a fish stew. Different regions have different versions. *Moqueca* from Bahia, for example, is African-influenced and uses palm oil, coconut milk and local fish.

Chimarrão

This hot drink is made from the leaves of the yerba mate tree. It is bright green, herby and creamy. The drink originated with Indigenous cultures, in particular the Guaraní and Tupi peoples.

Acarajé

This street food is a bean fritter that's fried and stuffed with spicy pastes or fillings like shrimp or vegetables. It has African origins and is often sold by Baianas: Afro-Brazilian women from Bahia.

BRIGADEIROS

ADULT SUPERVISION REQUIRED

These little chocolate balls are a popular treat in Brazil. They are often served at celebrations, like birthdays and weddings, or just as a simple treat! Some impatient people eat the chocolate mixture right out of the pot – this is known as *brigadeiro de colher* (spoon *brigadeiro*). This recipe makes about 30 *brigadeiros* to share.

Ingredients

- 397 g (14 oz) can of condensed milk
- 14 g (1 tbsp.) of butter
- 45 g (3 tbsp.) of cocoa powder (unsweetened)
- 65 g (⅓ cup) of sprinkles

Toppings

Try a few different toppings:
- Chocolate curls
- Chopped dried fruit
- Chopped nuts

Method

1. First, measure out your ingredients. Add the condensed milk, butter and cocoa powder to a medium-sized saucepan.
2. Turn the heat to medium. Stir the mixture slowly as it starts to melt.
3. Keep stirring constantly for 10 to 15 minutes until the mixture starts to thicken. Don't let it burn!

4. The mixture is thick enough when you can run your spoon through it to see the bottom of the pan and it takes about 3 seconds for the mixture to flow back into place.
5. Leave the mixture to fully cool.
6. Make the balls! When it's cool, use your hands to form the mixture into golf ball-sized balls. If it's too sticky, you can use a little bit of oil on your hands to make it easier.
7. On a clean, dry surface like a baking sheet, spread out a sheet of sprinkles. Roll each ball in the sprinkles.
8. Enjoy immediately or put in the fridge to keep cool.

 Be careful not to eat too much sugar in a day.

A brief history

The story goes that *brigadeiros* were named for Brigadier Eduardo Gomes (a brigadier is an army officer), who ran for **president** in the 1940s. People wanted to sell treats to raise money for his **election**, but ingredients like chocolate and fresh milk were hard to find after World War II. This recipe was invented using ingredients they could find easily.

CITIES, SCHOOLS AND INDUSTRY

São Paulo

Brazil is a huge country with diverse ways of living. About 88 per cent of the population live in cities, and Brazil has some of the biggest cities in the world. While some Indigenous people live in forests, savannahs and other natural spaces, some also live in urban areas.

Favelas

Many cities have areas of crowded housing called *favelas*. These developed as people moved to the cities in search of work. There was not enough access to housing, so people had to build their own. *Favelas* continue to grow today, and many lack consistent water and electricity supplies. *Favela* communities often have a strong art and cultural scene.

Farming

More than a third of all coffee in the world is produced in Brazil in one of the 300,000 **plantations**. Brazil also grows enormous amounts of soybeans, 75 per cent of which goes to feed animals on farms. Cattle farming is another major industry. Unfortunately, soybean and cattle farming result in huge amounts of deforestation.

Schools

School in Brazil is free until the age of 17. In many public schools (*escolas públicas*), the day is short and has two shifts: a morning shift runs from about 7:30am to about 12:30pm, and then afternoon students attend from about 1pm to 6pm. Some of the busiest schools even have lessons in the evening.

School stages

Infant:
4–6 years old

Elementary I:
6–10 years old

Elementary II:
10–14 years old

High:
15–17 years old

Tourism

Tourism is a booming sector in Brazil. An estimated 6.5 million people visit each year to sample the food, culture and climate. This feeds into businesses and the **economy**, but it can also have negative impacts on the environment and local communities.

IZABELA'S DAY

Name: Izabela Medeiros
Age: 11
Lives: São Paulo
Family: Mum, brother (Paulo), sister (Sophia)

Olá! My name is Izabela, and this is my day in year 5.

School starts at 7:30am so I get up at 6 and get ready. The sun is already up. I have cereal for breakfast and help my little brother Paulo get ready. My mum drives us to school before she goes to work. I help Paulo and Sophia with their things before I go to my classroom.

Sophia
(Younger sister)

Paulo
(Younger brother)

Me

Mum

I always sit with Carla and Bruno. When the bell rings at 7:30, the Portuguese teacher arrives. Today we write a pretend letter to make an argument about something. I am arguing that there are too many *telenovelas* in the evening. They are boring and should be aired later, when children have gone to bed.

Telenovela: A dramatic TV programme for adults.

Next, we have maths. We have a different teacher for each subject, and they come to our classroom when it is time for the class so we don't have to move.

After that, it's breaktime (*recreio*)! We go outside and have our snacks. I have a cheese sandwich and a banana and eat it quick so we can play football (*futebol*). We play King of the Street (*Rei da Rua*): the king is in goal and we take it in turns taking shots. If the king saves it, they stay in goal. If someone scores, they are in goal. Whoever is king the longest wins!

At 10 o'clock, the bells rings and we go back in for geography. We are making posters about deforestation. That's when trees are chopped down to make space for things like cattle farming. This is really bad because animals lose their homes and because the forests provide us with oxygen.

In the afternoon, we have history. History is my favourite because so much has happened! The last class is art. We have to clear away really well because in the afternoon a different set of pupils arrives to start their school day.

My mum comes to pick us up, and Bruno too because he's coming to my house. We have *arroz e feijão* with stewed chicken for lunch and then go to the park to meet my neighbours. Sophia comes too but Paulo always has a nap when it's hot after school. We put out goals but we only have six people so we play without anyone in goal. I'm practising dribbling with my left foot.

Arroz e feijão: Rice and beans. This is a common side dish.

When the sun starts to get really low, I know it's nearly time for Bruno's dad to get him, so we go back home. In October, the sun sets at around 6pm. When Bruno is gone, I do my homework and finish my letter for Portuguese class.

Farofa: A side dish of toasted cassava flour.

We all sit down at the table for dinner. We are having fish stew (*moqueca*) with rice and *farofa*.
We usually spend quite a long time eating and talking. Then Sophia and I play one of her educational video games while Paulo and Mum watch TV. I get ready for bed and read a bit and then it's time to sleep!

Good night (*boa noite*).

Fish stew (*moqueca*)

COLONISATION, FREEDOM, DEMOCRACY

People have existed in Brazil for at least 35,000 years. Before Europeans, Indigenous peoples like the Tupi and Guaraní were the biggest communities. It is estimated that between 2 and 11 million people were living in Brazil before contact with the Portuguese.

Pedro Álvares Cabral

Portuguese contact

The Portuguese arrived in 1500 CE, led by Pedro Álvares Cabral. Many Indigenous people were killed by warfare and diseases brought from Europe. The Portuguese established a **colony** and made attempts to enslave Indigenous people. They mined gold and diamonds and sent sugar and red dye back to Europe to sell.

FASCINATING FACT!

One of the oldest human skeletons found was discovered in a cave in Brazil. She was called Luzia and dated back 11,000 years.

Sugar plantation

Lei Áurea (Golden Law)

President Luiz Inácio Lula da Silva

Start of slavery

The Portuguese enslaved people from Africa to work on plantations. Brazil imported more than 5 million enslaved people over 300 years. Enslaved people survived and resisted by preserving their own languages, dances, music and food.

War of Independence

Prince Pedro I of Portugal was left to rule Brazil in 1820. In 1822, after the Brazilian people protested against Portuguese rule, Prince Pedro announced Brazil's independence. After three years of fighting, Portugal acknowledged Brazilian independence in 1825.

End of slavery and monarchy

The Golden Law abolished slavery in 1888, after decades of fighting by activists and *quilombos* (communities of escaped enslaved people). In 1889, the **monarchy** was overthrown by military leaders. This began the era of presidents.

Rise of democracy

Brazil suffered a series of corrupt leaders and **dictators** in the 1900s. Elections were often not fair or did not happen at all. In 1988, a new **constitution** gave people the right to vote in fair elections. Today, Brazil is a growing economy led by an elected president.

In the beginning there was no night. Only day.

HOW NIGHT CAME FROM THE OCEAN

The princess of the ocean left her underwater home to marry a prince of the land.

At first, they were happy. But the longer she stayed in the bright sun, the weaker she became.

I need the darkness of the deep ocean, but I am too weak to return to my father, the Great Sea Serpent.

I will send my brothers! Please, go to the Great Sea Serpent and ask for darkness for his daughter.

Yes!

Take this coconut. It is full of shadows. But be warned! Only my daughter can open it safely. SO NO PEEKING.

And so the brothers journeyed back with the coconut full of darkness. But something wasn't right.

I've never heard sounds like that.

What if it's a trap?

What if it's powerful?

We should peek!

But the Serpent said not to peek!

Yet peek, they did.

Ahhh...

In the darkness, the princess felt better at once.

But the darkness did not lift. The people grew frightened. Plants began to wilt and animals called out in distress.

HOOT
HOOT
GRRROWL

The princess knew she had to separate the night from the day, so she made a bird for the day.

You will sing for the dawn.

You will sing for the dusk.

And a bird for the night.

You three! You disobeyed the Great Sea Serpent and almost doomed us all!

POP
POP

The princess turned them into animals!

And so the cycle of night and day began.

FRUITS OF BRAZIL

From its many forests and jungles, Brazil has more than 300 different kinds of colourful, native fruits to offer. Read these tantalising descriptions of some of the fruits.

Maracujá

This is a plump oval fruit that can be pale orange, soft yellow, deep purple or green. Inside, the wet seeds have a sweet tropical flavour.

Caju

This bell-shaped fruit is stringy, juicy and has a sweet taste that's also a bit tangy. The olive-green cashew nut grows out of the top.

Jabuticaba

This firm, blackish-purple fruit looks similar to a grape, but has tougher, darker skin. Inside, the flesh is pearly white. It has a floral taste that's a bit peppery.

Guaraná

This has a hard, bumped shell that's a vibrant red. The fruit looks like an eye! It tastes slightly bitter.

Carambola

This is a long, ridged, star-shaped fruit. Its skin is waxy. It is sweet, citrussy and a bit sour.

What do the fruits taste like?
bitter, citrussy, floral, juicy, peppery, sour, sweet, tangy, tropical

How are the colours described?
black, deep, green, orange, pale, pearly, purple, red, vibrant, white, yellow

What textures are described?
bumped, firm, hard, plump, ridged, soft, stringy, tough, waxy, wet

Design your own fruit salad! Choose from the fruits above or add some of your favourites, such as strawberries or apples. Write a description of your fruit salad using the vocabulary boxes to help you.

- How do the different fruits look?
- How do they taste?

GLOSSARY

Abolished Officially ended.

Basalt Hard, black, volcanic rock.

Biodiversity Variety in plant and animal life.

Caiman A reptile related to the crocodile, but smaller than a crocodile.

Carbon dioxide A gas given off by using fossil fuels.

Colonisation The act of taking control of a land and settling by force, often displacing people who already exist there.

Colony A settlement created by people from another country or area.

Constitution A document that sets out the laws, beliefs and rules for a country.

Deforestation The clearing of forested areas.

Democracy A form of government in which the people in power are elected by the general population.

Dictator A ruler with total power over a country.

Echolocation The ability to locate items and environments using sound.

Ecological Relating to the environment and ecosystems.

Economy A system of making money and producing goods and services.

Ecosystem A community of plants, animals and other environmental factors that exist together and have relationships and interactions that affect each other.

Election A public vote.

Endangered At risk of extinction.

Endemic Native to a specific area or country and mainly or only found in that area or country.

Enslave To force someone to work for little or no pay and exclude them from human rights.

Equator An imaginary line around the Earth that is exactly halfway between the North and South Poles.

Erosion When wind, water, ice or other natural pressures wear away at rock.

Federal district A region of a country that is used as the base for the central government.

Hemisphere Regions north or south of the equator. There is the Northern Hemisphere and the Southern Hemisphere.

Heritage History, traditions, beliefs and practices that are inherited from the past.

Industry A particular area or type of business. For example, the automobile industry refers to the manufacture and sale of vehicles.

Monarchy A system of royalty with a head, such as a king or queen.

Mutualistic relationship When two organisms from different species work together beneficially for survival.

Plantation A farm or estate that grows a particular crop, such as coffee or bananas.

President An elected leader of a country. It can also mean the leader of an organisation or company.

Rainforest A tropical forest that gets a lot of rain.

Sandstone A rock formed from sand.

Subtropical Related to regions close to the tropics (the area around the equator), usually with mild-to-hot weather that changes with the seasons.

Tourism When people travel away from their home to see other places. The tourism industry involves travel, hotels, restaurants and attractions.

Tributaries Smaller water systems, like streams or small rivers, that flow into a larger water system, like a large river or lake.

Tropical Related to regions around the equator, usually with hot and humid weather all year.

Wetland Flooded area of land that is marshy and swampy.

INDEX

A

acarajé 27
African influences 19, 20, 21, 23, 27
Afro-Brazilians 19, 22, 23, 25, 27
agouties 16
Amazon rainforest 4, 5, 8, 9
Amazon River 5, 8, 14, 17
anacondas 15
Argentina 10
Atlantic Ocean 8, 9

B

Bahia 19, 25, 27
Baianas 25, 27
basalt 11
beaches 9, 20
biodiversity 5, 9
Black Consciousness Day 25
Bonfim 25
Brasília 4, 5, 6, 7
Brazil nut tree 16
brigadeiros 27, 28–29
butterflies 11

C

Cabral, Pedro Álvares 36
caimans 9, 14, 15, 16
Candomblé 22, 23
capoeira 21
capybaras 15
carbon dioxide 8, 44
Carnival (Carnaval) 19, 20, 24

cassava 26, 27, 35
Catholicism 22, 23, 25
celebrations 24–25, 28
Cerrado 9
chimarrão 27
cities 7, 25, 30
climate 8
coastline 9, 13
coffee production 31
colonisation 18, 19, 36
Corpus Christi 25
culture 18–21

D

deforestation 12, 13, 17, 31, 33, see also over-farming
democracy 37, 44
Devil's Throat 10
dictators 37, 44
dolphins 14
drinks 27

E

echolocation 14
ecosystem 17
education 31
endangered species 17
entertainment 20
European influences 19, 26
exports 6, 31

F

farming 9, 17, 31, 33
farofa 26, 35
fauna 6, 9, 11, 12–17

favelas 30
federal district 4, 7
feijoada 6, 26
flag 6, 7
flora 9, 15, 16
food 26–29, 42–43
football 19, 21, 33
forests 13, 11, 16, 17, 30 see also deforestation
fruits 42–43
futebol 21, 33

G

giant anteaters 11, 16
giant otters 17
golden lion tamarins 13
Gomes, Eduardo 29
governance 37
guaraná 27, 42
Guaraní 19, 27, 36

H

habitat loss 17
harpy eagles 13
history 36–37
hot lips (*Palicourea elata*) 17

I

Iguaçu Falls 5, 10–11
Iguaçu National Park 11
Iguaçu River 10, 11
independence 37
Independence Day 25
Indigenous peoples 18, 19, 22, 23, 26, 27, 30, 36
industries 31

J

jaguars 14, 16
jaguarundis 11
Japanese population 18

L

Lençóis Maranhenses
 National Park 9
Luzia 36

M

maned sloths 13
maned wolves 17
mixed martial arts (MMA) 21
monarchy 37
moqueca 27, 35

N

national dish 6, 26
national parks 9, 11

O

over-farming 9

P

pães de queijo 27
Pantanal 9, 14, 15, 17
Paraná Plateau 11
Pedro I 37
pink river dolphin 14
piranhas 14
plantations 31, 37
pollution 17
population distribution 30

Portugal 25
Portuguese language 7, 19, 21
Portuguese people 22, 36–37
presidents 37

Q

quilombos 37

R

rainforests 11, 13, 16, 17
 see also Amazon rainforest
red-bellied piranhas 14
religion 22–23
Rio de Janeiro 4, 7, 24
rufous-bellied thrush 6

S

samba 19, 20, 24
sandstone 11
Sateré-Mawé 27
savannahs 8, 9, 30
schools 31
Shamanism 23
slavery 23, 25, 36, 37
spiritualism 23
sports 21
Stairs Washing 25
states 4, 7

T

telenovelas 20, 32
terrains 8–9
toco toucans 12
tourism 31
trees 6, 8, 9, 16, 27

tributaries 8
Tupi 27, 36

U

Umbanda 22, 23

W

War of Independence 37
waterfalls 10–11
waterlilies, giant Amazon 15
wetlands 9, 14, 15, 17
work 31

Z

Zumbi dos Palmares 25

ACKNOWLEDGMENTS

The publisher would like to thank the following for their kind permission to reproduce their photographs:

(Key: a-above; b-below/bottom; c-centre; f-far; l-left; r-right; t-top)

Adobe Stock: Kushnirov Avraham 22, Sergey Bogomyako 9tr, marysckin 27clb, Lin V 24t, william87 37br; **Alamy Stock Photo:** James Berry 37tr, Chronicle 42tr, NTB 25cl, World History Archive 37cr; **Dreamstime.com:** Ab2147272 27tl, Ernest Akayeu 20tr, 28–29b (vegetables), 42–43 (Norse gods), F Baarssen 9cl, Natalia Chernyshova 7clb, Dmitry Chulov 11cla, Everst 21t, Frank Fichtmueller 13tl, Peter Hermes Furian 4cl, 4b, Boris Gavran 8, Aleksei Gorodenkov 31tl, Menno Van Der Haven 36, Jiri Hera 29bc, Andrei Hrabun 25bl, Oleksandra Klestova 33bc, Tetiana Kozachok 32-33 (Stationery), Dalia Kvedaraite 14b, Tomas Marek 11clb, Merfin 31ca, Igor Mojzes 21bl, Alexander Mychko 27cla, Nanisimova 10, Oksanabratanova 27bl, Roxxanna1 16tl, Vladimir Seliverstov 17tl, Shaiith 26t, Alexander Shalamov 21cl, Shapicingvar 6, Natalia Sokko 16cl, Oleksandr Sutchenko 31crb (x3), Adrian Szatewicz 9br, Stefano Zaccaria 30; **Getty Images:** The Image Bank Unreleased / Michel Setboun 23t; **Shutterstock.com:** Shpadaruk Aleksei 35r, Valda Butterworth 14tr, dreakrawi 19t, Ron Ellis 10b, everst 18, Andrey_Fokin 30b, Petros Goulas 25tl, GrumJum 28crb, Jan_Kuchar_Photo 16bl, Lyudmyla Kharlamova 28-29 (paper), 32tr, Lauritta 24b, lazydog20 7cl, Roland Magnusson 19cl, Borodacheva Marina 32-33 (Background), 34-35 (Background), Joe McDonald 15tl, Elizaveta Melentyeva 5, Muhammadphotoes 15cl, Hisa_Nishiya 32b, Konstantin Novikov 17tr, Nsit 28tr, Maciej Olszewski 14tl, Sofiia Popovych 34cb, Pro Symbols 26br, railway fx 6l, Risto Raunio 17b, Pavlo S 4br, See U in History 37cra, Simon's passion 4 Travel 23cl, SofieLion 12, Bjorn H Stuedal 13tr, Surajkalangada 26bl, David Pineda Svenske 20cl, Frederik Tellerup 19bl, Thx4Stock team 31clb (x2), TRphotos 7t, Tupungato 20br, urfin 29bl (cl), Sergey Uryadnikov 15bl, V. Belov 37crb, v.iraa 34-35 (Stickers), Karen Yomalli 13b

Cover images: *front:* **Getty Images:** Mike Hill br; **Getty Images / iStock:** lightpix cr, Nirut Punshiri t/ (Background); **Shutterstock.com:** *alaver bl; Back:* **Adobe Stock:** *Sergey Bogomyako tl, william87 bl;* **Shutterstock.com:** *SofieLion cl*

All of the books in the *Super World* series have been reviewed by authenticity readers of the cultures represented to make sure they are culturally accurate.